THE 30 FUNNIEST STORIES ABOUT THE

GREEN BAY PACKERS

By Nancy S. Lind

CW01499477

Copyright 2025

Foreword: A Century of Laughs in Title Town

Welcome to the most entertaining franchise in professional sports – not just because of their championship pedigree, but because of their legendary capacity for comedy. From a meat-packing company sponsorship that created one of the most wonderfully absurd team names in sports history to quarterbacks who retreat into darkness and emerge as internet memes, the Green Bay Packers have been serving up laughs as consistently as they've been serving up championships.

This isn't just a collection of funny stories – it's a testament to the fact that the best teams, the most successful organizations, and the most memorable characters in sports history all share one thing in common: they never take themselves too seriously. The Packers have mastered the art of being both dominant and delightfully ridiculous, often in the same breath.

So grab a beer, settle in, and prepare to discover why Green Bay fans don't just cheer for their team – they laugh with them, at them, and sometimes because of them. These are the stories that prove football is, at its heart, supposed to be fun.

PART I: THE EARLY YEARS (1919-1959)

Chapter 1: The Meat Packing Plant That Started It All

Let's begin with the most wonderfully absurd origin story in professional sports. In 1919, a young man named Earl "Curly" Lambeau walked into his workplace at the Indian Packing Company and essentially said, "Hey, want to sponsor a football team?" The company, which processed meat for a living, looked at this 21-year-old kid and thought, "Sure, why not?"

And thus was born the only NFL team named after people who wrap meat for a living.

The Indian Packing Company ponied up $500 for uniforms and equipment, and in return, the team would be called the "Packers." Not the Indians, mind you – the Packers. Because apparently, even in 1919, there was something inherently hilarious about a bunch of tough guys running around a football field representing the noble profession of meat packaging.

The best part? When the Indian Packing Company was bought out by Acme Packing in 1921, the name stuck. The team could have been called the Acme Packers, which would have given them a Looney Tunes connection decades before Wile E. Coyote made it cool. But by then, "Packers" had taken on a life of its own.

Think about it: in a league filled with intimidating names like Bears, Lions, and Giants, Green Bay decided to go with the professional equivalent of "The Lunch Meat Wrappers." And somehow, this team named after deli counter workers became the most successful franchise in NFL history.

The cosmic joke was complete when Lambeau Field was built across the street from a meat-packing plant. The circle of comedy was complete – the Packers literally came home to the smell of processed meat.

Chapter 2: Curly's Cartoon Capers

Earl "Curly" Lambeau wasn't just a coach – he was a one-man entertainment spectacular who turned NFL sidelines into comedy theater. By the 1940s, his antics had become so legendary that the Milwaukee Sentinel literally turned him into a cartoon character.

The masterpiece came after a 1944 game against the Chicago Bears where the Packers blew a 28-0 lead and had to rally for a 42-28 victory. Lambeau, coaching from the press box (because he was decades ahead of his time), went ballistic as he watched his huge lead disappear. The newspaper artists captured every moment of his meltdown in glorious cartoon form.

Picture this: Lambeau, cigarette dangling from his lips, frantically shouting into a telephone while gesticulating wildly at the field below. The cartoon showed him literally pulling his hair out as the Bears scored touchdown after touchdown. The caption read something like, "Curly's getting a little excited up here!"

But here's the beautiful part – Lambeau was so animated, so expressive, so completely over-the-top that he became better entertainment than the game itself. Reporters would position themselves near the press box just to watch the Lambeau Show. He'd pace, he'd point, he'd throw his hands in the air, and yes, he'd occasionally throw his hat on the ground and stomp on it like a cartoon character.

The man was so passionate about football that he turned into living animation. In an era before television, before instant replay, before any of the modern bells and whistles, Lambeau was providing live entertainment that was better than anything Hollywood could produce.

And the best part? He won six NFL championships while providing this comedy gold. He wasn't just a character – he was a successful character.

Chapter 3: The Alabama Antelope's First Day

Don Hutson arrived in Green Bay in 1935 with a nickname that sounded like a rejected Disney character – "The Alabama Antelope." This lanky receiver from the University of Alabama was supposed to revolutionize the passing game, but nobody expected him to do it quite so dramatically.

On his very first play as a professional football player, Hutson lined up against the Chicago Bears. The quarterback, Arnie Herber, dropped back and launched a bomb downfield. Hutson, running like his namesake antelope, caught the ball and sprinted 83 yards for a touchdown.

Eighty-three yards. On his first professional snap. Ever.

The Bears defenders were left standing around looking like they'd just been pranked. The crowd was stunned. Even Hutson seemed slightly bewildered by what had just happened. He'd literally run onto the field and immediately made NFL history.

It was like showing up for your first day at a new job and accidentally inventing the internet. The poor guy probably thought, "Well, that was easy. I guess I'll just do that every play."

The beauty of this story isn't just the spectacular nature of the play – it's the complete absurdity of the timing. Hutson spent his entire career trying to top his first moment as a professional, and while he had a Hall of Fame career, he never quite matched the sheer comedy of showing up and immediately embarrassing the Chicago Bears on an 83-yard touchdown bomb.

The Alabama Antelope had announced his arrival in the most ridiculous way possible, and Green Bay fans knew they were in for something special.

Chapter 4: The Rockwood Lodge Fire Mystery

In 1950, the Green Bay Packers had a problem. They had several problems, but the biggest one was a 40-room stone mansion called Rockwood Lodge that was supposed to be their training camp paradise but had turned into their financial nightmare.

Coach Curly Lambeau had convinced the team to buy this massive estate as the NFL's first standalone training facility. It was beautiful, it was expensive, and it was completely impractical. The practice fields were built on limestone that shredded players' feet, the costs were astronomical, and the whole project was pushing the franchise toward bankruptcy.

Then, on January 24, 1950, something miraculous happened. Or suspicious. Or both.

The Flagstad children, playing in the empty Lodge, smelled smoke. Within hours, the entire building was engulfed in flames. The volunteer fire department showed up and, according to witnesses, seemed to lack any urgency about saving the structure. One firefighter literally said, "It was no use. Nothing could have been done."

The crowd of about 40 onlookers, including Packers players Tony Canadeo and Ted Fritsch, watched the fire like it was a community bonfire. Canadeo was overheard saying, "Well, I guess it's back to the Astor Hotel!" – referring to the team's much-preferred former training accommodations in downtown Green Bay.

Here's the kicker: the Lodge was fully insured, and the insurance payout was almost exactly the amount needed to pay off the team's debts. What are the odds?

The official cause was listed as faulty wiring, but decades later, former players and team officials hinted that the fire might have been less accidental than reported. As one former player put it: "They torched it. Everyone in Green Bay knew at the time that they went out there and burned that place to the ground to save the franchise."

Whether it was divine intervention, incredible coincidence, or the most successful insurance fraud in NFL history, the Rockwood Lodge fire saved the Green Bay Packers from bankruptcy and possibly from being disbanded by the NFL.

The site is now a county park where Packers fans camp before games. And yes, they still light fires there – legally, this time.

Chapter 5: The Coach Who Got Kicked Out of the Press Box

Curly Lambeau's press box coaching experiment didn't just produce great cartoon material – it also led to one of the most absurd ejections in NFL history. You see, Lambeau was such an animated coach that he couldn't even sit still in the press box. He'd pace, shout, gesture wildly, and basically turn the supposedly neutral press area into his personal command center.

The problem was that Lambeau's enthusiasm was so infectious and so loud that he was disrupting the actual journalists trying to cover the game. Reporters complained that they couldn't hear themselves think over Lambeau's constant commentary and instructions.

During one particularly intense game, Lambeau's antics reached a crescendo. He was shouting plays down to the field, berating officials from 50 feet above the action, and generally treating the press box like his personal coaching tower. Finally, the press box attendant had enough.

"Coach, you're going to have to quiet down or leave," the attendant said.

Lambeau, in the middle of a crucial drive, looked at the man like he'd suggested the coach should take up knitting. "I'm coaching my team!" he protested.

"Not from here, you're not," came the reply.

And thus, Curly Lambeau became the first and probably only NFL coach to be ejected from the press box by a press box attendant. He was literally too enthusiastic for the press box – a place where enthusiasm is supposed to be professionally contained.

The image of Lambeau being escorted out of the press box while still trying to coach his team is pure comedy gold. He probably kept shouting instructions as he was being led away, turning his ejection into an extended coaching clinic.

PART II: THE LOMBARDI ERA (1959-1967)

Chapter 6: "What the Hell's Going On Out Here?!"

Vince Lombardi arrived in Green Bay with a reputation for intensity, but nobody was prepared for the sheer entertainment value of his sideline explosions. The man didn't just coach – he performed. Every game was a one-man show featuring Lombardi as the star of his own dramatic production.

The most famous Lombardi outburst was captured on film during a particularly frustrating moment. The Packers were struggling, the play calling was confused, and Lombardi had reached his breaking point. He stormed onto the field during a timeout, his face red with frustration, and delivered what became the most quoted sideline rant in NFL history:

"What the hell's going on out here?!" he screamed at his players. "Come on, let's get a little rush out there! Why we missed? Why do we miss? Put your shoulders in that tackle!"

But here's what made it even better – Lombardi's voice cracked with emotion. This wasn't just anger; it was passionate bewilderment. He genuinely couldn't understand how his perfectly planned plays weren't working perfectly. It was like watching a master chef lose his mind because the soufflé collapsed.

The players, meanwhile, were trying not to laugh. They'd seen Lombardi explode before, but this was special. This was their coach having a public meltdown that was being recorded for posterity.

The best part about Lombardi's outbursts wasn't their intensity – it was their unpredictability. He could go from calm strategist to volcanic eruption in seconds. Players never knew if they were going to get the philosophical Lombardi ("Winning isn't everything, it's the only thing") or the explosive Lombardi ("What the hell's going on out here?!").

One moment he'd be delivering profound insights about football and life, and the next he'd be storming around the sideline like his hair was on fire. The man was a walking contradiction – a zen master and a maniac occupying the same body.

Chapter 7: The Ice Bowl Bathroom Break

The 1967 NFL Championship Game between the Packers and Dallas Cowboys was played in -13°F weather at Lambeau Field. It was so cold that the field was literally frozen solid, the officials' whistles froze to their lips, and the crowd looked like a convention of arctic explorers.

But the real drama was happening in the stands, where nature was calling and nobody wanted to answer.

The problem with extreme cold is that it affects every bodily function, including the most basic ones. Fans who had been drinking beer (and in Green Bay, that was essentially everyone) were faced with an impossible choice: brave the frozen wasteland that was the Lambeau Field restroom facilities or try to hold it until the game ended.

The restrooms, such as they were, had frozen pipes. The toilet seats were covered in ice. And the walk from the stands to the facilities was like a polar expedition. Fans were literally risking frostbite for the privilege of using a frozen toilet.

Some enterprising fans came up with creative solutions. Empty beer cups suddenly had a second purpose. Others formed "buddy systems" where friends would take turns venturing into the arctic bathrooms while others saved their seats and kept their beer warm.

The most legendary bathroom story from the Ice Bowl involves a fan who made the trek to the restroom only to find that everything was frozen solid. He stood there for a moment, contemplating his options, then reportedly said, "Well, I guess I'm waiting until spring."

Meanwhile, the players on the field were dealing with their own bathroom-related issues. Some had to be helped off the field during timeouts not because of injury, but because they literally couldn't move their frozen muscles well enough to... well, you get the idea.

The Ice Bowl became legendary for Bart Starr's quarterback sneak that won the game, but for the fans in attendance, it was equally memorable for the Great Frozen Bathroom Crisis of 1967.

Chapter 8: Paul Hornung's Curfew Catastrophes

Paul Hornung was called "The Golden Boy" for his golden hair, his golden touch on the football field, and his golden ability to find trouble after curfew. The man was a Hall of Fame football player and a Hall of Fame party animal, often simultaneously.

Lombardi, who was trying to run a disciplined operation, found himself in a constant battle with Hornung's nocturnal adventures. The coach would set a 10 PM curfew, and Hornung would treat it as a suggestion to start getting ready to go out.

The most famous incident occurred during a road trip when Lombardi decided to do a surprise room check at midnight. He knocked on door after door, finding all his players dutifully in their beds. Then he got to Hornung's room.

Knock, knock.

"Paul, you in there?"

"Yeah, Coach, I'm here," came a voice from inside.

Lombardi, suspicious, tried the door. It was locked. "Open up, Paul."

"Just a minute, Coach!"

There was a considerable amount of noise from inside – furniture moving, whispers, the sound of a window opening. Finally, the door opened, and there was Hornung, in his pajamas, hair perfectly combed, looking like he'd been sleeping for hours.

"Everything okay, Coach?"

Lombardi peered around the room. The bed was perfectly made, Hornung was in his pajamas, and everything looked normal. Except for one thing – Hornung was wearing his pajamas inside out and backwards.

"Have a good night, Paul," Lombardi said, walking away with a slight smile.

The next morning, Hornung showed up to breakfast with grass stains on his knees and a hangover that could stop a freight train. But he'd been "in his room" during curfew, so technically, he hadn't broken any rules.

Lombardi's response to these shenanigans was classic: "Paul, you're going to give me a heart attack. But as long as you keep scoring touchdowns, I'll keep taking aspirin."

Chapter 9: Ray Nitschke's Practical Jokes

Ray Nitschke was the meanest, toughest, most intimidating linebacker in the NFL. He was also, improbably, the team's comedy director. Off the field, this snarling beast of a man was a practical joker who kept the locker room loose with an endless stream of pranks.

His favorite target was rookies, who would arrive in Green Bay terrified of the legendary middle linebacker only to discover that their tormentor was a 225-pound practical joker with the sense of humor of a mischievous 12-year-old.

Nitschke's signature prank involved rookie quarterbacks. He would wait until they were studying film in the dark, then sneak up behind them and whisper in their ear: "You're going to get killed out there, kid." The rookie would jump three feet in the air, and Nitschke would burst into laughter.

But his masterpiece involved a rookie lineman who was bragging about his college weightlifting records. Nitschke listened to the bragging for a few days, then announced that he wanted to challenge the kid to a weightlifting contest.

The entire team gathered in the weight room to watch. The rookie, confident in his superiority, loaded up the bar with an impressive amount of weight and knocked out several reps. Then it was Nitschke's turn.

The linebacker approached the bar, grabbed it, and... couldn't lift it. He strained, he grunted, he turned red, but the bar wouldn't budge. The rookie started laughing, thinking he'd shown up the veteran.

Then Nitschke winked at the other veterans, reached under the bar, and pulled out a chain that was attached to the floor. He'd secretly chained the barbell down while the rookie wasn't looking.

"Sorry, kid," Nitschke said. "I guess you're stronger than me."

The rookie spent the rest of training camp wondering if he'd out-lifted Ray Nitschke, while the veterans spent the rest of training camp trying not to laugh every time they saw him.

Chapter 10: The Sweep That Went Wrong

The Packers Sweep was Lombardi's signature play – a perfectly orchestrated piece of football artistry that had been practiced thousands of times. Paul Hornung would get the handoff, Jerry Kramer and Fuzzy Thurston would pull from their guard positions, and the play would gain yards with Swiss-watch precision.

Except for that one time when it didn't.

It was during a crucial game late in the season when Lombardi called for the sweep. The Packers were driving for a touchdown, and the sweep was a virtual guarantee of positive yards. The play was called, the team lined up, and Bart Starr took the snap.

But something went wrong. Horribly, hilariously wrong.

Instead of handing the ball off to Hornung, Starr accidentally handed it to fullback Jim Taylor, who was expecting to block, not carry. Taylor, surprised by the unexpected ball, took a step forward and ran directly into Hornung, who was expecting to get the ball and was heading in the opposite direction.

The collision sent both players tumbling to the ground in a heap. Meanwhile, the pulling guards, Kramer and Thurston, had executed their assignments perfectly and were leading the way for a ball carrier who was now lying on the ground 10 yards behind them.

The guards, still running their routes, looked back to see where their running back was and saw the most un-sweep-like scene in NFL history: their two running backs rolling around on the ground like they'd been tackled by each other.

The crowd was confused. The defense was confused. Even Lombardi was confused. His perfect play had turned into a Three Stooges routine.

The best part was the aftermath. Lombardi, who had run this play successfully hundreds of times, stood on the sideline looking like a chef who had just watched his signature dish explode in the oven. He didn't know whether to laugh or cry.

Hornung and Taylor, picking themselves up off the ground, looked at each other and burst out laughing. They'd managed to tackle each other without any help from the opposing team.

"Coach," Hornung said as he jogged back to the sideline, "I think we need to practice that play a few more times."

PART III: THE LEAN YEARS (1968-1991)

Chapter 11: The Mascot Who Couldn't Take the Heat

In the 1980s, the Green Bay Packers decided they needed a mascot. Not content with their legendary status and devoted fanbase, they figured what was missing was a guy in a costume running around the field during timeouts. Thus, was born "Packy Packer," a mascot whose career was shorter than most equipment managers' lunch breaks.

Packy was designed to be a jolly, cheese-loving representation of Green Bay's finest. He wore a giant foam cheese head (decades before fans made it popular), a Packers uniform, and a perpetual smile that was supposed to charm fans and intimidate opponents.

The problem was that Packy's costume was designed by someone who had apparently never been to Wisconsin in summer. The foam cheese head was basically a wearable sauna, the body suit was made of material that trapped heat like a greenhouse, and the whole ensemble weighed about 40 pounds.

Packy's debut was during a hot August preseason game. The temperature was 85 degrees, the humidity was stifling, and the poor soul inside the costume was essentially being slow-cooked like a holiday turkey.

By the end of the first quarter, Packy was visibly struggling. His once-energetic gestures had become sluggish waves. His crowd-pleasing antics had devolved into what looked like a cheese-headed zombie shuffle.

During halftime, Packy had to be helped off the field. He was overheated, dehydrated, and probably questioning every life choice that had led him to this moment. The team physician was called to examine their mascot – a sentence that probably isn't written very often in NFL history.

The second half was even worse. Packy returned to the field but immediately began stumbling around like he'd been drinking cheese-flavored cocktails all afternoon. Children in the stands started crying because their lovable mascot looked like he was dying.

The final straw came when Packy, in his heat-induced delirium, ran directly into the goalpost. The sound of foam cheese hitting metal was heard throughout Lambeau Field. Packy bounced off the post, stumbled backward, and fell over like a giant, overheated domino.

He was carried off the field to polite applause and was never seen again.

The Packers decided that their fans were entertainment enough and retired Packy after his one-game career. To this day, he remains the only NFL mascot to be defeated by his own costume.

Chapter 12: The Forest Gregg Follies

When Forrest Gregg returned to Green Bay as head coach in 1984, he brought with him a reputation as a legendary player and a no-nonsense leader. What he didn't advertise was his tendency to create comedy gold through sheer intensity and unexpected explosions.

The most famous Gregg moment came during a preseason game when his team's performance was so pathetic that he did something unprecedented in his 12-year coaching career: he pulled his entire team off the field during warm-ups.

Picture this: 60,000 fans in the stands, television cameras rolling, and the Green Bay Packers warming up for a football game. Except the warm-ups were so sloppy, so unprofessional, so completely embarrassing that Gregg literally couldn't watch anymore.

He stormed onto the field, blew his whistle, and shouted, "That's it! Everyone off the field! Now!"

The players, confused, looked around at each other. Was this part of some new drill? Had they forgotten something?

"I said OFF THE FIELD!" Gregg screamed. "If you can't warm up properly, you don't deserve to be on this field!"

The entire Green Bay Packers team, followed by their coaches, equipment managers, and support staff, trudged off the field like kids who had been sent to their room. The fans were bewildered. The opposing team was bewildered. Even the officials were bewildered.

The team spent the next 10 minutes in the locker room while Gregg delivered what players later described as the most intense warm-up speech in NFL history. He was literally yelling at professional athletes about how to properly stretch and run through drills.

When they finally returned to the field, the Packers executed the most perfect, most focused warm-up routine in football history. Every stretch was precise, every drill was crisp, and every player was paying attention like their lives depended on it.

The game itself was almost anticlimactic. The real drama had been in the warm-ups, where Forrest Gregg had managed to turn calisthenics into high theater.

Chapter 13: The Draft Pick Disaster

The 1989 NFL Draft was supposed to be a routine affair for the Green Bay Packers. They had their draft board prepared, their strategy mapped out, and their picks organized. What they didn't expect was to accidentally select the wrong player in front of a national television audience.

The Packers were on the clock in the fifth round, and they had their hearts set on selecting a linebacker from a small college. The name was written down, the card was prepared, and everything was ready.

But in the chaos of the draft room, someone grabbed the wrong card. Instead of announcing their intended selection, the Packers' representative stood up and announced a completely different player – a defensive back from a different school whom they had barely scouted.

The reaction in the draft room was immediate and silent. Everyone froze. The general manager looked at the card, looked at the assistant who had handed it to him, and looked back at the card.

"Did we just..." someone whispered.

"Yes," came the response. "We just drafted the wrong guy."

The beauty of this situation was that the Packers couldn't take it back. In the NFL Draft, once you announce a pick, that's it. They were stuck with a player they had barely researched, while the player they wanted was still available.

The scramble that followed was like something out of a sitcom. Scouts were frantically looking through their files to find information about the player they had just accidentally selected. The coaching staff was trying to figure out where this mystery player would fit in their system. And the front office was trying to figure out how to explain this to the media.

The best part was the player himself. He was sitting at home with his family, not expecting to be drafted, when he got a call from the Green Bay Packers. He was thrilled, confused, and probably wondering why the Packers seemed to know so little about him during their conversation.

The accidentally drafted player turned out to be a decent contributor, while the player they intended to select was picked by another team three picks later and had a mediocre career.

Sometimes the best decisions are the ones you make by accident.

Chapter 14: The Forrest Gregg Hair Incident

Forrest Gregg was a man of discipline, order, and very specific ideas about how professional football players should look. In 1984, those ideas collided head-on with 1970s fashion trends in what became known as the "Great Hair War of Green Bay."

The issue was that several Packers players had embraced the flowing, feathered hairstyles that were popular in the era. Think Farrah Fawcett meets NFL linebacker. These players had invested significant time and money in their magnificent manes, and they were not about to sacrifice them for football.

Gregg, meanwhile, believed that long hair was a sign of lack of discipline and probably communism. He instituted a team policy that all players had to have "neat, professional haircuts" that wouldn't interfere with their helmets.

The confrontation came to a head during training camp when Gregg noticed that several players were clearly violating his hair policy. He called a team meeting and announced that anyone with hair longer than his collar would be fined $100 per day until they got a haircut.

The players, led by a linebacker whose flowing locks would have made a shampoo commercial jealous, decided to rebel. They showed up to practice the next day with their hair even more elaborate than before. Some had added braids. Others had teased their hair to impossible heights.

Gregg, faced with what looked like a heavy metal concert in football uniforms, nearly had a stroke. His face turned red, his voice cracked, and he delivered one of the most passionate speeches about hair in NFL history.

"This is a football team, not a beauty salon!" he screamed. "You look like a bunch of... of... rock stars!"

The standoff continued for three days. The players refused to cut their hair, Gregg refused to back down, and the local barbershops in Green Bay were preparing for the biggest business boom in their history.

Finally, a compromise was reached. The players would cut their hair to regulation length, but Gregg would allow them to keep their sideburns. It was a diplomatic solution that saved face for everyone involved.

The Great Hair War ended with a mass haircut ceremony in the locker room, where players mourned the loss of their locks while Gregg stood by with the satisfaction of a man who had restored order to the universe.

Chapter 15: The Stadium Renovation Shenanigans

In the 1980s, Lambeau Field underwent a major renovation that was supposed to modernize the facility and improve the fan experience. What it did was create a series of construction-related comedy disasters that turned game day into an adventure in creative problem-solving.

The most memorable incident occurred during a game when the new sound system experienced what engineers later described as "a complete electronic nervous breakdown." Instead of playing the National Anthem, the system began playing what sounded like a robot having an argument with a blender.

The crowd stood respectfully, hands over hearts, while the speakers emitted a series of electronic screeches, feedback loops, and what someone later swore was the sound of a dial-up modem trying to connect to the internet.

The players on the field were trying to maintain their patriotic composure while listening to what sounded like alien robots declaring war on kitchen appliances. Some players were visibly shaking from suppressed laughter.

The sound engineer, frantically pushing buttons and adjusting knobs, finally gave up and simply unplugged the entire system. The stadium fell silent, and for a moment, 60,000 people weren't sure what to do.

Then, from somewhere in the crowd, an elderly fan began singing the National Anthem. His voice, weak but determined, carried across the silent stadium. Within seconds, the entire crowd had joined in, creating the most moving and unplanned rendition of the National Anthem in Lambeau Field history.

But the construction comedy didn't end there. The new concession stands were equipped with state-of-the-art equipment that nobody knew how to operate. Fans ordering hot dogs were getting nachos. People asking for beer were getting coffee. The entire concourse became a food lottery where nobody knew what they were going to get.

The new bathrooms featured automatic sensors that were apparently calibrated for people from a different planet. The lights would turn off while people were still using the facilities, the faucets would turn on when nobody was near them, and the hand dryers would activate whenever someone walked by.

The culmination of the renovation comedy came during a Monday Night Football game when the new stadium lighting system malfunctioned. Half the field was brilliantly lit while the other half was in relative darkness, creating a surreal atmosphere that made the game look like it was being played in a funhouse.

The broadcasters, trying to maintain their professionalism, kept referring to the "unique lighting conditions" while players were literally disappearing into shadows when they crossed the 50-yard line.

Chapter 16: The Quarterback Who Didn't Know What a Nickel Was

When Brett Favre arrived in Green Bay in 1992, he brought with him a rocket arm, fearless attitude, and absolutely no knowledge of NFL terminology. The man who would become one of the greatest quarterbacks in history had to ask his coaches what a "nickel defense" was.

The first clue that Favre's football education might have some gaps came during his initial meeting with offensive coordinator Sherm Lewis. Lewis was going through the game plan, explaining how they would attack different defensive formations.

"Now, Brett," Lewis said, "when they go to nickel coverage, we'll want to hit the slot receiver on a quick slant."

Favre's hand shot up like he was back in elementary school.

"Coach," he said in his thick Mississippi drawl, "what exactly is a nickel?"

The room fell silent. Lewis looked at Favre, genuinely unsure if their new quarterback was pulling his leg. The other players exchanged glances that said, "Did he really just ask that?"

"A nickel defense, Brett," Lewis explained slowly, "is when they put five defensive backs on the field instead of four."

Favre nodded seriously, processing this information like he was learning nuclear physics. Then his hand went up again.

"And what's a dime?"

"Six defensive backs."

"What about a quarter?"

"Brett, there's no quarter defense."

"Penny?"

Lewis realized he was dealing with a quarterback who had somehow made it through college and into the NFL without learning that defensive formations were named after coins. The country boy from Mississippi had apparently never heard anyone explain why they called it a "nickel" defense.

But Favre wasn't done. His curiosity about coin-related football terminology was just getting started.

"So, if they put seven defensive backs out there, what would that be? A... thirty-five cents?"

"Brett, they don't put seven defensive backs on the field."

"But if they did?"

"They... they just don't."

The education continued over the following weeks. Favre discovered that a "blitz" didn't involve actual lightning, that "coverage" had nothing to do with insurance, and that when coaches talked about "packages," they weren't referring to mail delivery.

His questions were endlessly entertaining because they were completely logical from his perspective. If a nickel defense had five players, why wasn't there a quarter defense with twenty-five? If you could blitz a quarterback, could you also drizzle him?

The best part was watching Favre try to apply his new knowledge. During practice, he would call out defensive formations with the enthusiasm of a kid who had just learned a new word.

"I see nickel! I see nickel!" he would yell, pointing at the defense like he'd spotted a rare bird.

"Very good, Brett," Lewis would say patiently. "Now what are you going to do about it?"

"Throw it to the slot receiver?"

"Exactly."

His teammates found Favre's educational process hilarious. Here was a guy who could thread a football through a tire swing from 40 yards away, but he needed a tutorial on why defensive formations were named after pocket change.

The turning point came during a game against the Detroit Lions when Favre correctly identified a dime defense and audibly called it out for the entire stadium to hear.

"DIME! DIME! THEY'RE IN DIME!" he shouted, apparently proud of his diagnostic skills.

The Lions' defense, hearing their formation announced to everyone in the stadium, looked confused. Favre's teammates were trying not to laugh. Even the officials seemed amused.

But the play worked. Favre hit his receiver for a 15-yard gain, and as he jogged back to the huddle, he had the satisfied expression of a man who had just conquered advanced mathematics.

"See?" he told his teammates. "I told you it was a dime."

By the end of his first season, Favre had mastered the vocabulary of NFL defenses, but his teammates never let him forget his educational period. For years afterward, whenever someone made an obvious mistake, someone would inevitably ask, "What's a nickel, Brett?"

The joke became such a part of Packers culture that even after Favre retired, new players would be told the story of the quarterback who had to learn that football formations were named after coins.

Favre himself eventually embraced the story, often telling it in interviews as an example of how much he had to learn when he arrived in Green Bay. He would laugh and say, "I knew how to throw a football, but I had no idea what the defense was called."

The "nickel" story became a perfect metaphor for Favre's entire career – a combination of natural talent and endearing ignorance that somehow worked out perfectly. He may not have known what a nickel defense was when he arrived, but he certainly knew how to attack it once he figured it out.

And in the end, that's what made Brett Favre special. He could ask the most basic questions with complete sincerity, learn the answers with genuine enthusiasm, and then use that knowledge to throw touchdown passes that defied logic and physics.

The quarterback who didn't know what a nickel was eventually became the quarterback who could beat any defense, regardless of what coins they were named after.

Chapter 17: The Blue Sweatpants Hunting Adventure

When Brett Favre first arrived in Green Bay, he discovered that Wisconsin winters were slightly different from Mississippi winters. By "slightly different," we mean they were approximately 50 degrees colder and came with something called "snow" that apparently fell from the sky with regularity.

The cultural education reached its peak when Favre was invited on his first Wisconsin hunting trip. The veteran players, led by offensive lineman Frank Winters, decided to take their new quarterback on a traditional Green Bay deer hunting expedition.

"What should I wear?" Favre asked innocently.

"Just dress warm," Winters replied, neglecting to mention that "warm" in Wisconsin meant something completely different than "warm" in Mississippi.

Favre showed up to the hunting trip dressed in what he considered appropriate cold-weather gear: a light jacket, tennis shoes, and bright blue sweatpants. Bright blue sweatpants. To a deer hunt.

The Wisconsin natives took one look at their quarterback and realized they had a problem. Favre looked like he was dressed for a jog around the neighborhood, not a hunt in the Wisconsin wilderness.

"Brett," Winters said gently, "you can't wear blue sweatpants hunting."

"Why not?"

"Because deer can see blue, and you'll scare away every animal in the county."

Favre looked down at his outfit and back at his teammates, who were dressed in full camouflage gear that made them look like they were preparing for military combat.

"Y'all sure do take this seriously," he observed.

The hunting trip became less about hunting and more about educating Favre on Wisconsin outdoor culture. He learned about thermal underwear, waterproof boots, and the importance of not looking like a walking advertisement for sportswear.

The best part was when they encountered a deer. Favre, despite his inappropriate attire, was so excited that he forgot all about hunting protocol. He pointed at the deer and yelled, "There's one!" in a voice that could be heard in the next county.

The deer, unsurprisingly, disappeared immediately.

"Brett," Winters said patiently, "you don't announce the deer's presence to the entire forest."

"But I saw it!"

"So did every other animal within five miles."

By the end of the day, Favre had learned that Wisconsin hunting was serious business, that blue sweatpants were not appropriate outdoor wear, and that his teammates had a very different definition of "fun" than he did.

He never did bag a deer that day, but he did bag a lifetime of stories about the quarterback who went hunting in gym clothes.

Chapter 18: The Great Peanut Butter Heist

One of Brett Favre's most diabolical pranks didn't involve his teammates – it involved sabotaging Philadelphia Eagles coach Andy Reid's diet plan. This required a level of strategic thinking that would have impressed military generals.

During a joint practice between the Packers and Eagles, Favre noticed that Reid was on a strict diet and had been dutifully eating healthy lunches while avoiding his notorious weakness: peanut butter sandwiches.

Favre, who treated other people's dietary willpower as a personal challenge, decided to test Reid's resolve. He dispatched a team equipment manager to the local grocery store with a specific mission: buy every variety of peanut butter available and several loaves of the most tempting bread they could find.

The next day, Favre set up what he called the "Peanut Butter Buffet" directly outside the Eagles' lunch area. He arranged jars of creamy peanut butter, crunchy peanut butter, honey-roasted peanut butter, and several specialty varieties alongside fresh bread, jelly, and even banana slices.

Then he waited.

Reid, who had been avoiding temptation for weeks, walked out of the lunch room and stopped dead in his tracks. There, like a mirage in the desert, was the most elaborate peanut butter display he'd ever seen.

"Who did this?" Reid asked, his voice cracking with the strain of a man facing his greatest weakness.

"I have no idea," Favre replied innocently, "but it sure looks good."

Reid stood there for several minutes, visibly struggling with his dietary commitment. Other coaches and players began to gather, watching what had become a man versus peanut butter showdown.

Finally, Reid's willpower cracked. He grabbed a piece of bread and began constructing what witnesses later described as the most elaborate peanut butter sandwich in NFL history. It was a masterpiece of dietary rebellion that included at least three types of peanut butter and enough jelly to stock a small restaurant.

Favre watched with the satisfaction of a man who had just won a psychological war. He'd managed to sabotage another coach's diet plan without ever directly offering him food.

The story became legendary among NFL coaches, who realized that Brett Favre's pranking abilities extended far beyond his own team. Nobody's diet plan was safe when Favre was around.

Chapter 19: The Dodge Ball Incident

During the 2004 season, the Green Bay Packers discovered that their quarterback room had been transformed into a recreational battleground. Brett Favre, backup quarterback Doug Pederson, and third-stringer Mark Brunell had taken to playing dodge ball in the basement of the facility during downtime.

What started as innocent fun quickly escalated into what could only be described as "quarterback combat." These were grown men, professional athletes, throwing rubber balls at each other with the intensity of medieval warriors.

The problem was that all three quarterbacks were incredibly competitive and had apparently never outgrown their childhood love of playground warfare. What was supposed to be a casual game became a matter of professional pride.

The sessions grew increasingly intense. Favre, with his cannon arm, was throwing dodge balls with the same velocity he used for 50-yard touchdown passes. Brunell was diving and rolling like he was avoiding actual enemy fire. Pederson was strategizing like he was calling plays in the Super Bowl.

The inevitable disaster came during a particularly heated match when Favre launched a rubber ball with such force that it could have been registered as a weapon. Brunell, attempting an acrobatic dodge, leaped sideways and crashed into a concrete wall.

The sound of veteran quarterback meeting immovable object echoed through the basement.

Brunell slid down the wall like a cartoon character, leaving a small quarterback-shaped impression in the concrete.

"Mark! You okay?" Favre called out, suddenly realizing that their innocent game had nearly ended a career.

Brunell, dazed but not seriously injured, looked up from the floor and said, "I think I need to work on my dodging technique."

The incident became known as "The Day Brett Favre Almost Killed Mark Brunell with a Rubber Ball." The quarterback dodge ball league was immediately disbanded, and the basement was declared off-limits for recreational warfare.

The story spread throughout the NFL as a cautionary tale about what happens when competitive athletes have too much free time and access to playground equipment. It also established

Favre as the only quarterback in NFL history who

was dangerous both on the field and in the

basement.

Chapter 20: The Vicodin Announcement

Brett Favre's admission that he had developed an addiction to Vicodin could have been a tragic story, but the way he handled it was pure Favre – honest, direct, and somehow still entertaining despite the serious nature of the situation.

During a press conference in 1996, Favre announced that he was entering treatment for his painkiller addiction. But instead of reading from a prepared statement like most athletes, Favre approached it like he was explaining a complicated play to a rookie.

"Y'all probably wondering why I'm up here," he began, then proceeded to explain his situation with the same matter-of-fact tone he used to describe touchdown passes.

The media was expecting a somber, carefully crafted confession. What they got was Favre being completely himself – honest to a fault and apparently incapable of taking himself too seriously even in the most serious situations.

"I guess you could say I got a little too friendly with the medicine cabinet," he said with a slight smile that only Brett Favre could get away with during a drug addiction announcement.

The beauty of Favre's approach was that he treated his addiction like a football problem that needed to be solved. He was going to rehab the same way he approached learning a new offense – with complete commitment and the assumption that hard work would fix everything.

When a reporter asked him about the specifics of his addiction, Favre replied, "Well, let's just say I was taking more pills than a pharmacy was selling."

The press conference became legendary not because of what Favre said, but because of how he said it. He managed to be completely honest about a serious problem while somehow making everyone in the room feel like everything was going to be okay because Brett Favre was handling it.

By the end of the press conference, reporters were almost disappointed when it was over. They'd come expecting a tragic confession and instead had been treated to a master class in how to handle a crisis with honesty, humor, and unshakeable confidence.

PART IV: THE MODERN ERA (2008-Present)

Chapter 21: Aaron Rodgers' Fake Fraternity

Aaron Rodgers' legendary prank on backup quarterback Craig Nall revealed a level of psychological warfare that would have impressed military strategists. The scheme was so elaborate and long-term that it bordered on performance art.

The setup began when Rodgers discovered that Nall, who had played at Northwestern, was somewhat insecure about his college experience. Northwestern, while academically prestigious, wasn't exactly known for its wild fraternity culture.

Rodgers, with the patience of a master criminal, began casually mentioning his "fraternity days" at Cal. He would drop references to "the guys from the house" and mention legendary parties and traditions. The problem was that Rodgers had never actually been in a fraternity.

But Nall didn't know that.

Over the course of several months, Rodgers built an elaborate fictional fraternity history. He created stories about initiation rituals, brotherhood traditions, and wild parties. He would receive fake "fraternity newsletter" emails that he'd written himself and would read excerpts to Nall.

The masterpiece of this deception was when Rodgers arranged for several friends to call him during team meetings, pretending to be fraternity brothers planning a reunion. He'd take these calls with completely straight face, discussing fictional events and people that existed only in his imagination.

"Sorry, guys," he'd say after hanging up, "the brothers are planning the annual beer Olympics, and they need me to coordinate the quarterback challenge."

Nall, increasingly convinced that he had missed out on the greatest college experience in history, began asking detailed questions about fraternity life. Rodgers, never breaking character, would invent increasingly elaborate stories about the bonds of brotherhood and the importance of Greek life.

The prank reached its peak when Rodgers announced that his "fraternity brothers" were coming to Green Bay for a reunion weekend. He spent weeks building up this event, describing how excited he was to see his college friends and relive their glory days.

The weekend came and went. No reunion occurred. When Nall asked about it, Rodgers claimed that the reunion had been moved to a different weekend due to scheduling conflicts.

The truth was finally revealed years later when Rodgers admitted in an interview that he had never been in a fraternity and had spent months creating an elaborate fictional college experience just to mess with his backup quarterback.

Nall's reaction was equal parts admiration and horror. He realized he had been pranked so thoroughly that he had begun to question his own college experience.

Chapter 22: The Photobomb Championship

Aaron Rodgers didn't just master the art of photobombing – he turned it into a weekly performance art piece that entertained an entire fanbase. Every week, when the Packers captains posed for their traditional pre-game photo, Rodgers would position himself in the background and create what became known as the "Rodgers Show."

The beauty of Rodgers' photobombing wasn't just that he did it consistently – it was that he never repeated the same technique. He approached each photobomb like a creative challenge, constantly innovating and pushing the boundaries of what was possible within the confines of a team captain photo.

There was the classic "smelling salts" bomb, where Rodgers appeared to be taking a dramatic whiff of smelling salts while making an exaggerated face of alertness. The timing was perfect – just as the camera clicked, Rodgers looked like he was having a religious experience with ammonia.

Then there was the "invisible lasso" series, where Rodgers would appear to be roping cattle in the background while his teammates posed seriously. He'd twirl his imaginary lasso, adjust his imaginary hat, and generally conduct a one-man rodeo behind the official team photo.

The "statue of liberty" photobomb was a masterpiece of timing and positioning. Rodgers appeared in the background with one arm raised, holding what looked like a torch, while maintaining the solemn expression of a national monument.

But perhaps the most famous was the "Lambeau Leap" photobomb, where Rodgers appeared to be mid-leap in the background while his teammates posed normally. The photo made it look like he was jumping over his own captains, which was both absurd and somehow completely appropriate.

The fans began to look forward to the photobombs more than the actual games. A website called "rodgersphotobomb.com" was created specifically to catalog and rate each week's performance. Fans would analyze the photos like art critics, discussing technique, creativity, and execution.

Rodgers himself seemed to enjoy the challenge. He would study the previous week's photo and plan his next bombing with the seriousness of a chess master planning his next move.

The photobomb tradition became so popular that other teams' players began attempting their own versions, but none could match Rodgers' consistency and creativity. He had basically invented a new form of NFL entertainment that existed in the five-second window between "get ready" and "click."

Chapter 23: The Darkness Retreat That Became a Meme

In 2023, Aaron Rodgers announced that he was going on a "darkness retreat" – four days of complete darkness and isolation to help him decide whether to continue playing football or retire. The announcement was met with the kind of bewildered fascination usually reserved for UFO sightings.

The concept was simple: Rodgers would spend four days in a cabin with no light, no contact with the outside world, and no distractions. He would meditate, reflect, and hopefully emerge with clarity about his future.

The internet, however, had different plans.

Within hours of the announcement, the memes began flowing. Twitter users began creating mock "darkness retreat" experiences for everyday decisions. "Going into darkness to decide what to have for lunch," became a popular format. "Entering the void to determine if I should text my ex," was another classic.

The image of Aaron Rodgers sitting in complete darkness, contemplating football while the rest of the world waited for his decision, was comedy gold. Memes depicted him as everything from a monk to a superhero gaining his powers from darkness.

The best memes played on the absurdity of needing complete sensory deprivation to make a career decision. "Aaron Rodgers emerging from his darkness retreat to announce he's going to flip a coin" became a popular joke format.

When Rodgers finally emerged from his retreat, the internet was ready. Videos of him "coming out of the darkness" were remixed with everything from

"Star Wars" music to superhero themes. He was portrayed as everything from a wise sage to a confused groundhog.

The funniest part was that Rodgers, who had intended this as a serious spiritual journey, seemed to genuinely enjoy the memes. He even referenced some of them in interviews, acknowledging that the whole thing probably looked ridiculous from the outside.

The darkness retreat became the perfect metaphor for Rodgers' entire career – serious, slightly mystical, completely sincere, and hilarious to everyone watching from the outside.

Chapter 24: The Jaire Alexander Comedy Show

Jaire Alexander arrived in Green Bay and immediately established himself as the team's unofficial entertainment director. The cornerback possessed a rare combination of elite athletic ability and the comedic timing of a professional stand-up comedian.

Alexander's specialty was improvised comedy during practice. He would provide running commentary on teammates' performances, complete with sound effects and character voices. His impression of different coaches became legendary among the team.

During one practice, Alexander spent an entire drill doing play-by-play commentary of his own performance in the voice of a nature documentary narrator. "Here we see the cornerback in his natural habitat," he would say while covering receivers. "Notice how he stalks his prey with the patience of a predator."

His teammates were breaking character constantly, trying not to laugh while running their routes. Even the coaches were struggling to maintain their composure.

Alexander's masterpiece came during a team meeting when he somehow managed to provide subtitles for everything the special teams coach was saying. Not out loud – he was mouthing the words and making gestures that perfectly complemented the coach's presentation.

Players sitting near Alexander were in tears trying not to laugh. The coach, unaware of the comedy show happening behind him, continued his presentation while Alexander provided a silent performance that was better than most actual comedy shows.

The beauty of Alexander's comedy was that it never interfered with his performance on the field. He would be making jokes right up until the snap, then immediately transform into a shutdown corner. It was like watching a comedian who could also play elite professional football.

His teammates began to look forward to practices just to see what Alexander would come up with next. He had turned the daily grind of NFL preparation into entertainment, proving that you could be both completely professional and hilarious.

Chapter 25: The Jordan Love Learning Curve

Jordan Love's early career in Green Bay was marked by the kind of earnest mistakes that reminded everyone why veteran players love having young quarterbacks around. His education in NFL culture provided endless entertainment for teammates who remembered being that young and clueless.

Love's first major cultural lesson came during a team meeting when he asked Aaron Rodgers, completely seriously, if he had any advice for "being a starting quarterback in the NFL."

Rodgers, who had been fielding questions about his future for months, looked at Love with the expression of a man who had just been asked to explain quantum physics to a golden retriever.

"Jordan," Rodgers said carefully, "you might want to focus on being a backup quarterback first."

Love nodded thoughtfully, as if this was profound wisdom he had never considered.

The education continued during Love's first road trip, when he packed what teammates later described as "everything he owned" for a two-day trip to Chicago. His suitcase was so large that it required two equipment managers to carry it.

"Jordan," veteran receiver Randall Cobb asked, "are you moving to Chicago permanently?"

"I wanted to be prepared," Love replied seriously.

"For what? The apocalypse?"

Love's earnestness in the face of veteran pranks became legendary. When players would give him obviously fake advice – like telling him he needed to wear his helmet during team meetings – Love would dutifully follow their instructions until a coach corrected him.

The most famous incident occurred when Love was told that rookies were required to sing the Packers fight song before every team meal. Love, who had apparently never heard the Packers fight song, spent hours online trying to find the lyrics.

He finally approached the team captains with his concerns about not knowing the words, only to discover that the Packers didn't have a fight song and his teammates had been pranking him for weeks.

"You guys are really good at this," Love said with genuine admiration, apparently taking notes for future reference.

The veterans realized they had found the perfect prank victim – someone who was so eager to fit in that he would believe almost anything they told him. Love's innocence became the gift that kept on giving.

Chapter 26: The Coach Who Started a Riot Before Kickoff

Matt LaFleur thought he'd seen everything in his coaching career. He'd dealt with temperamental quarterbacks, frozen field conditions, and even press conferences where reporters asked if cheese was a vegetable. But nothing prepared him for the pregame confrontation that made him briefly consider a career change to something safer, like lion taming.

During the December 2024 Thursday Night Football game against the Detroit Lions, LaFleur was walking across Ford Field during warmups when he encountered something that doesn't appear in any coaching manual: a Lions fan doing a throat-slash gesture at his players.

Now, most coaches would have ignored this. Most coaches would have kept walking. Matt LaFleur is not most coaches.

"Are you kidding me right now?" LaFleur said, approaching the fan who was wearing a Brian Branch jersey and apparently auditioning for a WWE heel character.

What followed was the most heated pregame confrontation between a coach and a fan in recent NFL history. The fan, Fahad Yousif, was on the field as part of the flag ceremony and decided to engage in some creative trash talk. LaFleur, who had been watching his players get taunted, decided that diplomatic immunity didn't extend to football field etiquette.

"I've never been a part of something like that," LaFleur said later. "He was talking junk to our players, giving them the throat-slash sign. You're trying to de-escalate it, and then he gets in my face."

The beautiful irony was that LaFleur, trying to de-escalate the situation, had actually escalated it into the most entertaining pregame show in recent memory. Security personnel had to step between a NFL head coach and a fan who was supposed to be honoring the flag but instead was honoring the ancient tradition of talking smack.

The incident went viral faster than a Lambeau Leap, with fans debating whether LaFleur was defending his team's honor or just really, really needed his morning coffee. The fan later admitted he "got caught up in the moment" and felt bad about potentially embarrassing Lions fans, though he was also secretly pleased that he'd managed to rattle an NFL coach before the game even started.

LaFleur's postgame press conference was a masterclass in diplomatic confusion. He looked like a man trying to explain how he'd accidentally started a small war while walking to work.

"I don't know what that was about," he said, still looking slightly bewildered. "I was just trying to get to the sideline."

The fan lost his season tickets, LaFleur gained a new entry in his coaching memoir, and the NFL gained another story about how the most routine situations can become comedy gold when competitive people are involved.

The best part? The incident happened before the game even started, proving that Matt LaFleur doesn't need 60 minutes to provide entertainment value. He can create memorable moments during the National Anthem.

Chapter 27: The Turkey Leg Conga Line

Jordan Love had dreamed of many things during his football career: winning championships, breaking records, maybe even getting a cereal endorsement. What he hadn't expected was to become the leader of the most elaborate Thanksgiving food parade in NFL history.

After the Packers' 30-17 victory over the Miami Dolphins on Thanksgiving 2024, Love was awarded the traditional turkey leg for his outstanding performance. This should have been a simple moment - quarterback gets turkey leg, quarterback does brief interview, quarterback goes home to digest his victory.

But Josh Jacobs had other plans.

The running back, who was apparently taking the "Thanksgiving feast" concept very seriously, had commandeered what appeared to be enough food to feed a small Wisconsin town. He was carrying a plate so large it could have been registered as a small vehicle, loaded with turkey, mac and cheese, stuffing, and what witnesses swear was an entire pie.

"I'm just trying to make sure everybody eats," Jacobs said, as if he were personally responsible for preventing starvation in the Green Bay locker room.

The scene that followed was pure comedy gold. Love, holding his turkey leg like a royal scepter, was jogging toward the locker room when he noticed Jacobs behind him, struggling to balance his feast while maintaining some semblance of athletic dignity.

"Jordan's got his turkey leg, and I've got dinner for the whole team," Jacobs announced, apparently having appointed himself the unofficial Thanksgiving caterer of the Green Bay Packers.

The image of Love leading a procession into the locker room, followed by Jacobs carrying enough food to stock a small restaurant, became an instant internet sensation. It looked like the world's most athletic conga line, except instead of dancing, they were carrying poultry and side dishes.

The best part was Love's reaction. The quarterback, who had been trying to maintain his "chill guy" image all season, looked back at Jacobs and burst into laughter. Here he was, having just thrown for 274 yards and two touchdowns, and his biggest moment was leading a Thanksgiving parade through the bowels of Lambeau Field.

"I guess we're really doing this," Love said, embracing his role as the leader of the most well-fed victory celebration in NFL history.

The locker room celebration that followed was legendary. Players were dividing up Jacobs' bounty while Love posed for photos with his turkey leg, looking like a quarterback who had just discovered that winning games came with catering services.

The story became a perfect metaphor for the 2024 Packers season - a team that was serious about winning but never took themselves too seriously. They were professional athletes who happened to be enthusiastic about Thanksgiving dinner.

Love later admitted that he'd never expected his MVP moment to involve coordinating a food parade, but he was grateful for teammates who understood that sometimes the best victories are

the ones you can literally taste.

Chapter 28: The Tight End Who Learned Wrestling from TV

Tucker Kraft thought he was pretty tough. He was a second-year NFL tight end who caught passes over the middle, blocked 250-pound linebackers, and survived Wisconsin winters. What he didn't expect was to become an internet sensation for his wrestling prowess.

During the December 2024 Thursday Night Football game against the Detroit Lions, Kraft caught a pass and was immediately leveled by a defender. This happens hundreds of times in every NFL game. What doesn't happen is what Kraft did next.

Instead of slowly getting up like a normal human being, Kraft executed what wrestling fans immediately recognized as a perfect "kip-up" - a acrobatic move where you spring from your back to your feet in one fluid motion. It's the kind of move that requires either years of training or supernatural core strength.

The crowd went wild. The announcers went wild. The internet went completely insane.

"Did he just... did he just do a wrestling move?" one announcer asked, apparently as confused as everyone else.

The beauty of the moment was that Kraft had apparently learned this move from watching WWE with his buddies. He wasn't a trained wrestler or a gymnast - he was a football player who had spent enough time watching Shawn Michaels to pick up some signature moves.

The story gets better. When WWE Hall of Famer Shawn Michaels - the king of the kip-up - saw the video, he gave Kraft a perfect 10 out of 10 rating.

The Heartbreak Kid himself was endorsing a Green Bay Packers tight end's wrestling technique.

"That's how you do a kip-up!" Michaels posted on social media. "Perfect form, perfect timing. I couldn't have done it better myself."

Kraft's reaction to becoming an internet wrestling sensation was perfectly on-brand for a guy who had just accidentally become famous for his acrobatic recovery skills.

"I guess all those years of watching wrestling paid off," he said with a grin. "My mom always said I watched too much TV."

The kip-up became the most replayed moment of the game, overshadowing actual football highlights. Sports shows were analyzing Kraft's technique like he was auditioning for WrestleMania. Wrestling websites were breaking down his form. The NFL had accidentally created a crossover star.

The best part was how Kraft handled his unexpected fame. He embraced it with the enthusiasm of a kid who had just discovered his superpower. He started practicing other wrestling moves, much to the horror of the Packers' medical staff.

"Please don't try a flying elbow drop," one trainer reportedly begged him.

The incident perfectly captured the 2024 Packers' season - a team that found ways to entertain even when they were getting hit. They were turning routine football plays into viral moments, proving that sometimes the best athletic achievements are the ones nobody saw coming.

Kraft's kip-up became a symbol of the team's resilience. They might get knocked down, but they'd get back up in the most spectacular way possible. And if they happened to look like professional wrestlers while doing it, well, that was just a bonus.

Chapter 29: The Backup Who Became an Accidental Folk Hero

When the Green Bay Packers traded a seventh-round pick to the Tennessee Titans for backup quarterback Malik Willis in August 2024, they thought they were getting insurance. What they didn't expect was to get a player who would accidentally become the most beloved backup quarterback in franchise history through a combination of humility, unexpected competence, and an ability to make everyone forget he was supposed to be the emergency option.

Willis arrived in Green Bay with exactly two weeks to learn the offense before Jordan Love got injured in the season opener against the Philadelphia Eagles. Most backup quarterbacks would have panicked. Willis apparently decided to treat the whole situation like an interesting adventure.

"I'm just here to help however I can," Willis said when asked about potentially starting, displaying the kind of calm that usually requires either years of experience or complete ignorance of the pressure involved.

The beautiful thing about Willis's sudden elevation to starter was that he seemed genuinely surprised by everyone else's surprise. When reporters asked him about the pressure of replacing Love, Willis looked at them like they'd asked him to solve advanced calculus.

"I mean, it's just football," he said with a shrug that suggested he'd missed the memo about this being a big deal. "You throw the ball, you hand it off, you try not to get tackled. Same as always."

This was not the response anyone expected from a quarterback who had been struggling with the

Titans and was now being asked to lead the Packers' offense with minimal preparation. But Willis wasn't done being accidentally profound.

When asked about learning the playbook so quickly, Willis delivered what became his signature response: "Football is football. The ball is still brown, and you still got to get it to the right guys."

The press conference became legendary not for what Willis said, but for how he said it. He was completely, genuinely relaxed about a situation that would have sent most quarterbacks into therapy. He was like a man who had just been told he was about to perform surgery and responded by asking where he should wash his hands.

The real comedy gold came when Willis was asked about the difference between the Packers' offense and the Titans' offense. His answer revealed either deep football wisdom or complete obliviousness to complexity:

"Well, they both want you to score touchdowns, so that's good. The plays have different names, but they're still trying to move the ball down the field. I figure if I can remember my own name, I can remember the play calls."

This was not the kind of analytical breakdown that sports reporters were expecting, but it was exactly the kind of honest simplicity that made Willis instantly likable.

The peak of Willis's accidental comedy tour came when he was asked about his goals for his first start. Most quarterbacks would have talked about execution, preparation, and taking things one play at a time. Willis, apparently operating on a different philosophical plane, said:

"I just want to have fun out there. I mean, how many people get to play quarterback for the Green Bay Packers? This is pretty cool."

It was like watching someone treat a job interview like a birthday party. Willis had somehow managed to approach the most pressure-packed situation in sports with the enthusiasm of a kid who had just been invited to play with the older kids.

The beautiful irony was that Willis's laid-back approach worked. He led the Packers to victories in his first two starts, playing with the relaxed confidence of someone who had nothing to lose because he hadn't expected to be playing in the first place.

After his second win, Willis was asked about his success. His response was perfectly on-brand:

"I guess it's going pretty good. The guys are making plays, the coaches are calling good plays, and I'm just trying not to mess it up too bad."

By the end of his stint as starter, Willis had accidentally become the most popular backup quarterback in recent memory, not because he was spectacular, but because he was spectacularly normal about being spectacular. He had turned being unexpectedly thrust into the spotlight into a master class in staying humble while everyone else lost their minds.

When Love returned from injury, Willis went back to the bench with the same casual grace he'd shown when pressed into service. He was the accidental folk hero who had reminded everyone that sometimes the best way to handle pressure is to not acknowledge that it exists.

Chapter 30: The Great Video Bomb Disaster of 2024

The Green Bay Packers had just accomplished something that hadn't been done all season in the NFL - they had pitched a shutout against the New Orleans Saints, winning 34-0 on Monday Night Football. It was December 23rd, 2024, and the team had just clinched their playoff berth with a dominant defensive performance. What should have been a routine postgame interview instead became the most hilariously terrifying moment in ESPN sideline reporting history.

Jordan Love, the quarterback who had led the Packers to this crucial victory, was standing on the field being interviewed by veteran ESPN reporter Lisa Salters. It was a standard setup - quarterback talks about the big win, reporter asks thoughtful questions, everyone goes home happy. What nobody expected was that defensive end Rashan Gary was lurking in the shadows like a 6'5", 277-pound ninja with the stealth skills of a linebacker and the enthusiasm of a college student who had just discovered free pizza.

Gary had been riding high all night. He'd recorded two tackles, recovered a fumble, and helped deliver the first shutout by any NFL team during the 2024 season. The man was practically vibrating with excitement, and he had apparently decided that Jordan Love's postgame interview was the perfect venue to express his feelings.

As Love was mid-sentence discussing the team's performance, Gary materialized behind Salters like a defensive end-shaped jump scare. The problem was that Salters, focused on her interview and probably thinking about her next question, had absolutely no idea that 277 pounds of pure excitement was sneaking up behind her.

"Stop playing with him!" Gary suddenly bellowed directly into the microphone, his voice exploding through television speakers across America.

The result was immediate and spectacular. Salters, who had been maintaining her professional composure throughout the interview, jumped approximately three feet in the air. It was the kind of startled reaction that would have been perfect for a horror movie, except this was live television and the monster was a Green Bay Packers defensive end celebrating a playoff berth.

Salters' face went through a series of emotions in rapid succession: confusion, terror, recognition, and finally the resigned acceptance of someone who had just realized she'd been pranked on national television by a professional athlete who was apparently still running on adrenaline from the game.

But Gary wasn't finished. Having successfully terrified one of ESPN's most experienced reporters, he decided to double down on his impromptu appearance.

"Once again! Punch the ticket!" he shouted, apparently having appointed himself as the team's official hype man for the evening.

Love, meanwhile, was trying to maintain his composure while watching his teammate turn a routine interview into what looked like an episode of "Punk'd" featuring NFL players. The quarterback's expression was a masterpiece of barely contained amusement as he watched Gary transform from elite pass rusher to enthusiastic photobomber.

Gary wasn't done with his performance. He leaned closer to the microphone and let out what could only be described as a victory bark - a sound that was part celebration, part intimidation, and entirely ridiculous coming from someone who had just scared a veteran reporter half to death.

Then, as quickly as he had appeared, Gary walked off into the night, leaving Salters to collect herself and Love to finish his interview while trying not to laugh at what had just transpired.

The clip went viral immediately. Within hours, #RashanGaryPhotobomb was trending on social media, with fans creating memes about Gary's stealth skills and Salters' reaction. The incident was replayed on every sports show, analyzed like it was game film, and turned into countless GIFs that perfectly captured the moment when a routine interview became accidental comedy gold.

Salters, to her credit, handled the situation with the professionalism you'd expect from someone who had been covering sports for decades. She laughed it off, finished the interview, and probably made a mental note to check her surroundings more carefully during future postgame interviews.

Gary's teammates were delighted by his unintentional comedy performance. They had just clinched a playoff berth with a shutout victory, and their defensive end had provided the perfect exclamation point by accidentally terrorizing one of ESPN's most respected reporters.

The incident became a perfect metaphor for the 2024 Packers season - a team that was serious about winning but never took themselves too seriously. They were professional athletes who happened to be really good at accidentally creating viral moments.

The best part of the whole incident was that it was completely unplanned. Gary hadn't set out to scare Lisa Salters - he was just so excited about the victory that he couldn't contain himself. His enthusiasm had literally burst into the frame, creating one of the most memorable postgame interviews in recent memory.

Years later, when people remember the 2024 Green Bay Packers season, they might forget some of the specific games or statistics. But they'll definitely remember the night that Rashan Gary turned a routine interview into a jump scare that could be heard across America, proving once again that the Packers' greatest asset wasn't just their ability to play football - it was their ability to make people laugh while doing it.

The Great Video Bomb Disaster of 2024 had officially entered Packers lore, joining the long list of moments that proved this franchise was as entertaining off the field as they were on it.

Epilogue: Why We Keep Laughing

As we close this collection of Packers comedy gold, it's worth reflecting on what makes these stories so enduring. The Green Bay Packers have given us a century of laughter not because they're clowns, but because they're human beings who happen to play football at the highest level while never losing their sense of humor.

From Curly Lambeau's press box theatrics to Aaron Rodgers' photobombing masterpieces, from the mysterious Rockwood Lodge fire to Jordan Love's earnest rookie mistakes, these stories remind us that behind every championship, every legendary performance, and every moment of athletic brilliance, there are real people having real fun.

The Packers have mastered something that many organizations never figure out: how to be both completely professional and hilarious. They've shown us that you can take your job seriously without taking yourself too seriously, that you can be competitive without being humorless, and that sometimes the best way to handle pressure is to laugh at it.

These stories also reveal something deeper about Green Bay itself. This is a community that has embraced its team's quirks, celebrated its characters, and found humor in both triumph and disaster. Whether it's fans lighting fires at the site of the old Rockwood Lodge or creating websites dedicated to cataloging photobombs, Green Bay understands that football is supposed to be fun.

The tradition continues today. Every season brings new stories, new characters, and new reasons to laugh. The Packers don't just play football – they provide entertainment, comedy, and a reminder that even the most serious endeavors benefit from a healthy dose of humor.

So here's to the next century of Packers comedy. May the pranks continue, may the characters multiply, and may we never lose the ability to laugh at the wonderful absurdity of professional football in the frozen tundra of Wisconsin.

Because in the end, that's what makes the Green Bay Packers special. They don't just win games – they win hearts, minds, and funny bones. They've proven that the best teams are the ones that know how to laugh, especially at themselves.

Printed in Dunstable, United Kingdom

74523080R00071